Praise

For anyone
a difference with limited resources, this book is a
powerful reminder that even the smallest efforts can
spark significant change. Catherine Curry-Williams
has crafted more than just a guide; she has created an
inspiring call to action.

~ Joyce Mandell, President, Andrew J.
and Joyce D. Mandell Family Foundation, Inc.

It takes fearless women to get the job done. And few
are more fearless and committed than Catherine
Curry-Williams. Her brand of generosity is
contagious. It's also therapeutic. Bottom line: once you
read this book, you'll find there are no longer excuses
to fulfill that long-awaited desire to make the world a
better place.

~Roma Torre, TV journalist and theater critic

This inspiring book nudges all of us to take action
to lift up women and girls in our world! It reminds
us that everyone can do something to add value.
Catherine's message is exactly what the world needs to
hear right now.

~Julie Peterson Klein,
EVP | Chief Culture Office Bell Bank

Philanthropy on a Shoestring

HOW TO MAKE A DIFFERENCE ON $1.40 A DAY

Catherine Curry-Williams

The Three Tomatoes Book Publishing

Published September 2024

ISBN: 979-8-9903014-8-1
Library of Congress Control Number: 2024915905

For information address:
The Three Tomatoes Book Publishing
6 Soundview Rd.
Glen Cove, NY 11542

Cover design: David Harel
Interior design: Susan Herbst
Author Photo: Kathy Schuh

Dedication

This book is dedicated to all the fearless trailblazers, past and present, known and unknown, who have fought and continue to fight for equality for women— this is for you. Your strength, perseverance, and vision pave the way for a brighter future for us all. Your courage and unwavering dedication inspire me every day.

*Never doubt that a small group of thoughtful,
committed citizens can change the world.
Indeed, it is the only thing that ever has.*

~Margaret Meade

Table of Contents

My journey from despair to purposeful living.

Preface

March 28, 1997 will forever be carved in my heart as a day of immense joy and profound sorrow. It was a day that began with endless possibilities, brimming with hope and anticipation. I had been married for a year and eagerly awaiting my first child's arrival. When the news came that we were to have a boy, we were overjoyed.

We had meticulously prepared for his arrival, ensuring every detail was perfect. His clothes, carriage, and crib were all ready and waiting. We painted his bedroom multiple times, in various shades of blue. And as for his name, we had chosen Shane—a name that held deep meaning, signifying "God is gracious" in Irish and "Gift from God" in Hebrew.

I went into labor at thirty-nine weeks, and everything went pretty much as planned. Ice chips, breathing, and inspirational music in the background. After six hours and one final push, Shane entered the world.

But our joy quickly turned to confusion and fear as Shane struggled to take his first breath. The doctor's efforts to stimulate him yielded no response, and, before we knew it, a team of nurses rushed in, whisking our precious baby away, leaving us reeling in shock.

For nine agonizing days, we watched helplessly as our beautiful six-pound, seven-ounce baby boy lay in the confines of the NICU, surrounded by a tangle of tubes and wires. Each day brought new uncertainties, new fears, and yet no answers. I pumped breast milk in hopes of nourishing him. I cradled him in my arms, dressed him, brushed his hair, and talked sweetly in his ear. He looked so perfect, and he smelled like honey. I barely left his side. I spent hours trying to understand why this was happening and, at the same time, loving him like I had never loved anyone in my whole life.

On the tenth day, Shane was diagnosed with a rare genetic disorder—spinal muscular atrophy. I couldn't believe what I was hearing. The best-case scenario was that Shane would spend his life in a wheelchair.

The worst-case scenario is what happened; Shane lived for only two weeks. It was incomprehensible; we were completely devastated. How could this be happening?

The news shattered us, leaving us adrift in grief and despair.

The aftermath of losing Shane is almost impossible to sum up in words. In my darkest moments, from the rocking chair of Shane's empty bedroom, I wrote love letters to him in heaven and many furious letters to God. Somehow, I thought I could make sense of this and find meaning in the deep pain in my heart. Many days, I thought I would not be able to continue. I felt hopeless.

Six months after Shane had passed away, I received a letter from my sister-in-law Miriam, who lived three thousand miles away. She was reading a newspaper article when she saw a story about a woman whose child had recently passed from the same rare genetic disorder as Shane. I knew I had to talk to this woman. I did some research, found her number, and called her on the spot. We talked for hours, consoling each other. She told me about her son, who was nine months old when he passed away, and how she was inspired to do something good in his memory. At that moment, I felt my first glimmer of hope. It was like a tiny spark in the darkness, a possibility that urged me to keep going. The possibility of transforming this piercing pain into something meaningful, something that would help others and be a tribute to Shane's memory.

I began to channel my pain into purpose.

With the unwavering support of my community, Shane's Inspiration was founded—an organization dedicated to building the first universally accessible playground in the western United States. A place where children with disabilities and their able-bodied peers could play side by side, fostering inclusivity. A place where Shane would've been able to play alongside his friends in his wheelchair.

As Shane's Inspiration blossomed, so did our mission. What began as a local endeavor burgeoned into a global inclusion movement, spanning continents and transcending boundaries. Today, we have over eighty playgrounds on five continents and education programs in thirty countries in five languages. Little did I know

Catherine Curry-Williams

that this spark of hope would grow into a worldwide inclusion movement.

This was all beyond my wildest dreams. I never imagined this would be where I am today.

I knew nothing about philanthropy, building playgrounds, raising millions of dollars, or gathering teams of volunteers.

I was born in the heart of Bensonhurst, Brooklyn, the youngest of four sisters. My dreams seemed distant, and the odds of realizing them seemed stacked against me. I didn't excel in school like my sisters. I figuratively and literally danced as fast as possible to prove my worth. My parents were divorced by the time I was nine. My mom had multiple jobs to provide for us, and I became a latchkey kid. By age fourteen, I had a fake ID so I could get into bars. My main goal at the time was to be able to get into a disco and not get arrested.

I left Brooklyn and ventured to Hollywood to do what every eighteen-year-old girl without a plan does. I waited tables by day and went to acting classes at night. I found some success doing television commercials, but it was hardly the career I had envisioned. And, like many dreams, things materialized differently. Life had other plans for me.

Through the loss of my son and then the birth of my daughter, Grace, I began to see the world through new eyes.

In 2020, I was doing some research when I came upon a startling piece of information that shook me to my core: women and girls receive less than 1.8 percent of all US charitable giving. I searched and searched for information to disprove this data. Unfortunately, there was none. Women's and girls' initiatives were not even on the index charts until about 2016 when the Lilly family foundation did the first index. I was outraged.

At this point, I realized that inclusion wasn't only for playgrounds.

The information I learned about the inequity in the nonprofit sector about women and girls receiving less than animals made me angry. I thought, Where would I be today without the support of all those women in my life? But I knew full well that just being angry wouldn't help. So, I got into action. The first thing I did was call several of my very close girlfriends to tell them. They also did some deep diving into the statistics and were surprised to learn this fact was true. At that point, we called a few more friends. And then, finally, the answer was apparent to us—we would need to start our own organization.

She Angels Foundation began in July 2020 during the pandemic—an organization empowering women and girls across diverse communities. We are a collective giving organization that raises funds specifically through our Collective Giving membership. A hundred percent of our membership donations go directly to our grant-awarding program, giving grants to a broad portfolio of women's and girls' foundations that provide mentorship, funding, and resources to women's and girls' causes.

In a short span of four years, She Angels Foundation has awarded more than forty-five $5,000 grants, which have impacted thousands of women across our country.

Each step forward we take is a step toward a more equitable world for women and girls.

In 2024, we began our second program. The Philanthropy Circles Program aims to educate and mentor young women across the United States on the effectiveness and impact of collective giving and to increase support for female-led nonprofits.

She Angels Foundation believes that teaching young women about collective giving, mentorship, and community engagement will create a swell of philanthropy for women and girls in our country.

Recognizing that everyone's journey is different, it's important to find what personally motivates us and where we can best channel our efforts for growth and transformation.

My life has been a series of twists and turns, guiding me to this very moment. Amid the challenges and setbacks, I unearthed a reservoir of inner strength.

Who would have imagined that the determination that once propelled a carefree teenager into the world of discos would later become my superpower, encouraging me to navigate through the depths of sorrow and emerge stronger than ever before?

Catherine Curry-Williams

Visualize a world where philanthropy isn't reserved for the wealthy.

1

Challenging Conventional Concepts of Philanthropy

A world where anyone, even you, can make a significant impact with as little as $1.40 a day. Sounds impossible? Let's disrupt that notion together by challenging the conventional concepts of giving and showing that true change comes from passion, commitment, and a bit of creativity.

The World Needs Your Light

The world can often feel chaotic and filled with stress and fear. But here's the thing—you have a choice. You can either get lost in the chaos or look for the love, peace, and unity that still exists. It's time to shift our focus and become beacons of light in our communities. Reflect on where you're putting your time and attention. Are you complaining about the state of the world, or are you re-solving issues? Are you walking your talk, or just venting about injustices?

Don't Wait for Millions

You don't need to have millions to make a change. Start with what you have. Don't put things on the back burner waiting for a perfect time. The perfect time is now.

You can become a leader in your community with just a small, consistent effort.

Be a Disrupter

Forget what you thought you knew about philanthropy. Disrupt the scarcity mind-set and embrace abundance. We all have the potential to give, but we need to practice an abundant mind-set. My motto is simple—see the light, be the light, and share the light. Begin by believing in yourself and the possibilities. Then, share your light with others.

Think of the powerful women who disrupt their fields:

- Take Megan Rapinoe, for instance. She's a professional soccer player and captain of the US Women's National Team. Megan uses her platform to drive significant conversations and change in sports and beyond.
- Marley Dias started the #1000BlackGirlBooks campaign when she was just eleven years old. Marley saw a lack of diversity in the books she was reading and decided to do something about it. Her initiative has collected thousands of books featuring Black girls as main characters and inspired

many young people to make a difference.

- Or consider Amanda Gorman, the youngest inaugural poet in US history. Amanda uses her powerful words to address social issues like gender equality and racial justice. She also founded One Pen One Page, a nonprofit that promotes literacy and creativity among underserved youth.
- And then there's Jane Fonda, actress, political activist, feminist, environmentalist. She has lent her celebrity to the climate crisis and started the Fire Drill Fridays—Take Action with Jane, Greenpeace USA and the #FireDrillFriday movement!

These women are amazing, right? You don't have to be famous to be a disrupter. Whether you're sixteen or eighty-six you can be an everyday hero or disruptor. Think about your own community. Maybe there's a girl or a woman who started a recycling program or someone who volunteers at the local shelter. They're breaking down barriers and showing that anyone can contribute, regardless of their financial status or fame. It's about challenging old ideas and showing that giving back isn't just for the wealthy.

Don't wait until you have it all figured out. Start now and grow along the way.

Perfection in Progress
Perfection isn't about getting everything right the first

time. It's about constant improvement. As women, we are equal contenders in the realm of giving. Our core values, passion, and persistence are what make us strong.

Responsibility isn't a burden. It's a privilege to be a part of something bigger than yourself.

Embrace Responsibility

I'm not suggesting we completely reinvent the wheel of philanthropy. But I am absolutely sure that we need to shake it up and challenge it and challenge ourselves. Embrace the responsibility that comes with being a part of your community. Take what works, build on it, and infuse it with your unique spirit.

Step into Your Power

Join the movement of philanthropists on a shoestring and prove that making a difference doesn't require a fortune—just a heart full of love and a mindset on change.

The key is to start. Jump on the bandwagon and make it fun. Challenge yourself and your friends to see the big picture.

With $1.40 a day, you can light up the world, one small step at a time.

Catherine Curry-Williams

**Getting real.
The world of
giving has some
serious power,
especially for
women and
girls.**

2

The Power of Philanthropy

First, let's clarify the difference between charity and philanthropy. Charity can be just a Band-Aid for immediate crises—think Hurricane Katrina, the devastation in Puerto Rico, or the aftermath of 9/11. We dive into our pockets, driven by our hearts and emotions, to help those in dire need. I'm not saying a Band-Aid isn't important.

Philanthropy, on the other hand, is the love of humanity on a whole new level. It's about playing the long game—strategic, thoughtful, and deliberate giving to causes we care deeply about.

This means digging into the real needs of underserved communities or championing causes that hit home—like education, health, domestic violence, or gender equality. Strategic giving is about backing organizations that are hustling to make lasting change.

So, what does strategic giving look like? It's about

channeling your efforts where they'll pack the biggest punch. Do your homework, pick causes that vibe with your values, and look for clear, measurable goals. Instead of just tossing money into a general fund, you might support a program that trains women in leadership or offers scholarships for girls in STEM. This way, your donations are more than just cash—they're catalysts for change.

Julia Boorstin nails it in her book *When Women Lead*. She points out that women often excel at strategic philanthropy because we're all about long-term solutions and sustainable change.

Invest in what matters to you and keep at it. You're not just making a one-off donation—you're planting seeds for a better future.

Now, let's talk about the perks of philanthropy—not just for those on the receiving end, but for us givers, too. Ever felt that warm, fuzzy glow when you've helped someone out? That's not just in your head—it's science!

The Perks of Philanthropy

Boosts Your Mood

Giving can seriously lift your spirits. Studies show that acts of kindness, like donating money or volunteering, trigger your brain to release feel-good chemicals like dopamine and endorphins. It's like a natural high, leaving you with a sense of fulfillment and joy. And honestly, in these wild times, who couldn't use an extra dose of joy?

Reduces Stress
Helping others can actually chill you out. When you focus on someone else's needs, your own worries tend to take a back seat. Research suggests that being charitable can lower stress levels, helping you to relax and feel more at peace.

Improves Physical Health
Believe it or not, philanthropy can give your physical health a boost, too. One study published in *The Journal of Health Psychology* found that people who donated money had lower blood pressure compared to those who didn't. So, giving back isn't just good for the soul—it's good for the body.

Enhances Social Connections
Philanthropy often means connecting with others. For women and girls, these social ties are gold. They give us a sense of belonging and support, fighting off loneliness and isolation. Strong social connections are linked to a longer life—research from Brigham Young University and UNC Chapel Hill found that people with solid relationships had a 50 percent better survival rate than those with weaker ties.

Catherine Curry-Williams

5 Fosters Gratitude

Giving back makes you appreciate what you have. It shifts your focus from what's missing in your life to what you can offer. Cultivating gratitude is linked to greater happiness and life satisfaction.

So, by diving into philanthropy, you're not just making the world a better place—you're potentially adding years to your life!

Your generosity doesn't just impact others; it boomerangs back to boost your health, well-being, and happiness.

Catherine Curry-Williams

Collective giving offers an outstanding opportunity to maximize impact.

3

Building a Collective Giving Circle

Pooling your resources and talents can lead to some serious magic. Creating a giving circle is like assembling your own dream team, or if you prefer to call it your squad, all united by the mission to make the world a better place. By combining your resources and enthusiasm with others who share your values, you can achieve way more together than you ever could solo.

Think about it: a powerhouse of ideas, projects, and positive impacts, all born from a shared vision of a better world. In fact, a study by the Collective Giving Research Group found that giving circles have exploded recently, involving over one hundred and fifty thousand people

Engaging in collective giving can address immediate needs and lay the foundation for long-term change, leaving a legacy of compassion and generosity for future generations.

Catherine Curry-Williams

and donating around $1.29 billion. Not surprisingly, 70 percent of those giving circle members are women, showing just how crucial we are in this collective philanthropy game.

Benefits of Collective Giving

Strength in Numbers
When we band together for a cause, our impact is way bigger than the sum of our parts. By uniting under a common goal, we can leverage our combined resources and skills to create massive change.

Diverse Perspectives
Giving circles bring together people from all sorts of backgrounds, professions, and experiences. This mix fuels creativity and innovation. For women, it means pooling a wide array of insights and approaches to tackle the issues that matter most.

Shared Purpose and Passion
My fave. Collective giving gives women passionate about philanthropy a platform to connect and collaborate. This shared enthusiasm is like rocket fuel, supercharging the collective commitment.

4 ### Building Community

One of the coolest things about collective giving is the sense of belonging and camaraderie among participants. It's not just about philanthropy; it's about forming meaningful connections and friendships that empower and support each other.

5 ### Long-Term Sustainability

Collective giving initiatives build a community of supporters united by a shared mission, laying the groundwork for lasting impact. This creates a legacy women can be proud of. Take the Women's Giving Alliance in Jacksonville, Florida—they've granted over $6 million since 2001 to local nonprofits focused on women's issues. This sustained support has tackled education, health care, and economic empowerment, proving how women's collective philanthropy can drive lasting, positive change.

She Angels Foundation is another powerhouse, funding female-founded nonprofits that address social issues, supporting gender equality, education, and women's health.

With some thoughtful planning and open dialogue, your circle can blossom into a nurturing community of kindness and goodwill.

How to Start Your Own Collective Giving Circle

Here are Some Tips

Collective Giving Gathering

Round up your friends, family, and neighbors—especially those who share your passion for giving—and kick off your party of kindness and compassion. Watch it create a ripple effect of positive change.

Find a chill spot to gather.

Be picky about who you invite. Look for like-minded women who share your values and are fired up about making a difference. Diversity in backgrounds, perspectives, and skills is key.

Set the values that will guide your circle.

 Start small; eight to ten people are perfect for a cozy vibe and making everyone feel special.

 Make sure everyone knows the circle's purpose and goals.

 Create a supportive environment where everyone feels comfortable sharing their ideas, concerns, and suggestions.

 Snacks are a must! Water, wine, tea—whatever suits your crew. Finger foods are great for keeping the conversation flowing while you nibble and brainstorm ways to change the world.

Stories

Have everyone share their stories and visions for why supporting a specific cause matters to them. Discuss where they first learned about charity and giving. Initiate conversations from childhood and what their experiences have been so far with charitable giving. Ask them their perspective and what they thought it would take for them to be a philanthropist. This way you know where everyone is coming from and you can together dispel myths and create your own challenge of conventional concepts of philanthropy.

Money

Alright, here's the deal—you need to agree on an annual contribution from each member. This isn't just about the cash—it's about planning and setting yourselves up for success. Figuring out everyone's annual contribution helps you get a clear picture of your donation potential. Think about it—if everyone chips in, you'll know exactly how much money you'll have to play with by the end of the year.

Now, you don't have to put all your eggs in one basket. Maybe you want to spread the love a bit. You can decide to support two or even more organizations and split your funds. It's all about your creativity and what you, as a group, think will make the most

Catherine Curry-Williams

impact. Maybe one cause tugs at your heart-strings more, or you want to diversify your impact. Whatever floats your boat!

And hey, remember, these are just suggestions. Feel free to tweak them, add your own flair, and make them better. There's no one-size-fits-all answer here. This is a guide, not a rule book. You do you!

Beyond Money

Sure, fundraising is the bread and butter, but don't underestimate the power of raising awareness. Get loud about your cause. Use your social media game to spread the word. Host events, create buzz, and get people talking.

Sometimes, raising awareness can be just as impactful as raising funds. You're not just building a piggy bank— you're building a movement.

By getting the word out, you're educating others, rallying more supporters, and creating a ripple effect of positive change. So, whether it's through Instagram stories, TikTok videos, or good old-fashioned word of mouth, make sure people know what you're about and why it matters.

Grassroots organizations are the real MVPs, making a huge impact with what little they have.

Supporting Grassroots Organizations

In my opinion, grassroots organizations are the real deal. They're out there, in the trenches, rolling up their sleeves and getting stuff done to create positive change in their communities and beyond.

These organizations are powered by a diverse crew of folks dedicated to making things better. And at the heart of these movements? Women. Their leadership, empathy, and resilience are transforming communities left and right.

Women in grassroots organizations bring something special to the table. Their involvement isn't just beneficial—it's a game changer. Studies show that when women step up in leadership roles, the impact goes through the roof. Their hard work breaks down barriers, gives a voice to the voiceless, and sparks real change. Women in these roles don't just lead; they light up the room with their passion and dedication, making sure their movements are heard and felt deeply within their communities.

Take, for instance, the countless women-led grassroots movements addressing issues like domestic violence, education inequality, and environmental justice. These women aren't waiting for permission to act; they're mobilizing their communities, creating support networks, and demanding change. Their grassroots initiatives have led to new shelters for victims of domestic violence, after-school programs that keep kids off the streets, and community gardens that provide fresh food in urban food deserts.

Women's involvement is a powerhouse in grassroots organizations. Their contributions don't just shape the narrative; they turn dreams of a better world into reality.

Unlike bigger organizations, grassroots groups rely heavily on volunteers who selflessly give their time and expertise. These volunteers are the heartbeat of the organization, keeping the mission alive with their unwavering dedication.

Plus, the money invested in grassroots organizations stretches further. With minimal administration costs or overhead, every cent counts and makes a big impact on the ground.

Although I wholeheartedly believe in organizations finding the best person for the job and paying higher wages and salaries to attract top talent, I also recognize the importance of efficient resource use in grassroots organizations. Enter Dan Pallotta—a big advocate for rethinking how we approach charity and nonprofit work.

Dan Pallotta is known for his TED talk, "The Way We Think About Charity is Dead Wrong," which has sparked conversations about how we value and compensate nonprofit work. Pallotta argues that the nonprofit sector suffers from a double standard when it comes to compensation. While the for-profit sector can attract top talent with competitive salaries, nonprofits are often criticized for offering similar compensation. Pallotta believes that this mind-set hinders nonprofits from achieving their full potential because they can't attract the best and brightest to lead their causes.

He champions the idea that nonprofits should be able to invest in their own growth, including spending on advertising, marketing, and high salaries for top executives, just like for-profit businesses. He argues that by doing so, nonprofits can scale their impact, reach more people, and solve bigger problems. Pallotta's perspective challenges the traditional views on overhead costs, suggesting that these investments are crucial for growth and sustainability.

However, while Pallotta's arguments make a compelling case for investing in talent and growth, grassroots organizations often operate with limited funds. They maximize their impact by keeping administrative

Catherine Curry-Williams

costs low and relying heavily on volunteers. This means that every dollar donated goes directly into action, making visible and immediate changes in the community.

That said, it's important to find a balance. While grassroots organizations excel with their efficient use of funds, recognizing the need for fair compensation and growth investments in the nonprofit sector is equally crucial.

The goal is to create a sustainable model where both small grassroots efforts and larger nonprofit organizations can thrive.

So, while we celebrate the efficiency and direct impact of grassroots organizations, it's also essential to support a broader understanding of nonprofit success—a view that includes fair wages, investment in growth, and the potential to attract top talent. By doing so, we can ensure that all levels of nonprofit work are equipped to make a difference.

> *Grassroots movements are sprouting up everywhere like wildflowers, each one a testament to the power of collective action.*

Recent data shows there are tens of thousands of grassroots organizations worldwide, each tackling unique challenges in their communities. From fighting for clean water in Flint, Michigan, to advocating for LGBTQ+ rights in small towns, these movements are diverse and dynamic.

These organizations are breaking down barriers, giving a platform to marginalized voices, and driving meaningful change.

Grassroots organizations embody the spirit of community-driven philanthropy. They represent hope, resilience, and solidarity in a world that often feels uncertain.

One of the coolest things about grassroots movements is their ability to shake things up. They operate outside traditional structures, which allows for innovation and experimentation. They're all about flexibility, adaptability, and taking calculated risks.

This agility lets grassroots organizations respond quickly to emerging needs in their communities. They are, without a doubt, at the forefront of change. For example, during the COVID-19 pandemic, many grassroots groups quickly mobilized to provide masks, food, and support to vulnerable populations long before larger organizations could respond.

Grassroots movements also cultivate a sense of ownership among community members. When people are directly involved in decision-making, they feel a deeper connection to the cause. This ownership fuels passion and commitment, leading to long-lasting impact.

In essence, grassroots organizations embody grassroots democracy—a belief that power should be with the people. They empower individuals to become agents of change, promoting collective responsibility and solidarity.

But let's keep it real. Grassroots organizations face big hurdles in getting funding.

Big donors often have criteria that leave smaller organizations out in the cold. For instance, while MacKenzie Scott's philanthropic efforts are awesome, they target organizations with budgets over

$1 million. This leaves many grassroots organizations scrambling despite their potential for huge impact. In the world of philanthropy, big money tends to go to big organizations, leaving the little guys to hustle twice as hard. This disparity highlights the need to advocate for fair funding opportunities that uplift grassroots initiatives and make sure all voices are heard and supported in the quest for positive change.

By now, it's clear why I'm all about championing grassroots organizations and their efforts.

Together, we can amplify their voices, support their initiatives, and build a future based on empathy, justice, and compassion.

In today's world, where equity and inclusion are the talk of the town, you'd think we'd be nailing it by now.

What is DEI&B, Women, and the Gaps

But nope, the stats show we've still got a long way to go in hitting those DEI&B (Diversity, Equity, Inclusion, and Belonging) targets, especially for women in the US. It's high time organizations up their game in promoting gender diversity, tackling those pesky microaggressions, and crafting work environments that actually support and flex for everyone.

Nonprofits play a *huge* role in driving DEI&B. They're often at the forefront, pushing for social change and providing resources to underserved communities.

Breaking Down DEI&B for Women

Diversity

Boosting gender diversity means getting more women into various fields and leadership roles. It's about recognizing the unique perspectives women bring from all walks of life—different races, ethnicities, sexual orientations, and economic backgrounds.

Equity

2

Let's talk about fairness. Tackling the systemic inequalities women face, like wage gaps and career hurdles, is a must. We need policies that support work-life balance—parental leave, flexible hours, and childcare. And let's not forget mentorship and professional development opportunities tailored for women.

Inclusion

3

I know a lot about inclusion. As the founder of the nonprofit organization Shane's Inspiration, where we created one of the first initiatives in a worldwide inclusion movement for children with disabilities, I realize today that there is a critical need for inclusion in all areas, not just playgrounds.

> *Creating an inclusive workplace where women feel valued and heard is nonnegotiable.*

Women's voices should echo in decision-making processes, and their contributions should shine. We also have to stomp out harassment, discrimination, and bias in all settings.

4 Belonging

Belonging is the secret of true inclusion. It's not just about having a seat at the table; it's about feeling comfy and valued in that seat. It means crafting an environment where women can be their true selves without the fear of judgment. We need to actively listen, celebrate their wins, and support them through the rough patches.

**Belonging isn't just a buzzword;
it's a controversial yet crucial aspect of DEI&B.**

Many companies talk a big game about inclusion but often miss the mark on creating genuine belonging. This isn't about token gestures; it's about a deep-rooted commitment to transforming organizational culture so everyone feels genuinely accepted and valued.

Addressing these issues and cultivating a true sense of belonging can boost employee satisfaction, performance, and retention. This, in turn, creates a more innovative and resilient workplace. But if we ignore these underlying issues, all our inclusion efforts might feel pretty hollow.

Catherine Curry-Williams

Connecting DEI&B with Philanthropy

DEI&B can totally transform the way we think about philanthropy.

Support Diverse Causes

1 Put your money where it matters! Focus on nonprofits that are all about DEI&B. Your dollars will help create a world where everyone feels included and valued.

Volunteer Inclusively

2 Your time is just as powerful as your cash. Find organizations that push for equity and inclusion and get involved. You'll be part of a movement that's making real changes.

Advocate for Equity

3 Speak up! Whether it's in your job, your community, or on social media, use your voice to promote policies that support fairness. Your advocacy can light the spark for big changes.

Mentor and Support

4 Be a mentor and offer support to women and marginalized groups. Share your experiences and help break down barriers. You'll be paving the way for more inclusive opportunities.

By integrating DEI&B into your philanthropic efforts, you're boosting these organizations and their missions. When nonprofits thrive, so do the communities they serve.

The DEI&B Landscape for Women in the US

Let's dive into some cold, hard facts about where the US stands on DEI&B for women in the workplace:

1 *Leadership Representation*
Only 11 percent of companies in the Russell 3000 index have gender-balanced boards, and many have minimal or zero female representation.

Women of color are even more underrepresented, with just 3 percent being Black, 2 percent Asian, 1 percent Hispanic, and a tiny 0.03 percent Indigenous.

Only 24% of CEOs globally are women. We've made some progress, but there's still a mountain to climb.

2 *Workplace Challenges*
Women, especially those from marginalized groups, endure microaggressions and psycho-

logical stress at work. This leads to higher burn-out rates and more women contemplating quitting.

Flexible work arrangements are gold for women juggling childcare and household duties.

Yet, many companies still favor on-site work, creating a disconnect between what employees need and what the bosses think is best.

3 **_Impact on Innovation and Productivity_**
Companies with less diverse leadership are less likely to champion the ideas of women and people of color.

Women in these settings are 20 percent less likely to have their ideas endorsed compared to their male counterparts.

This stifles innovation and creates a less inclusive workplace culture.

Let's ensure every woman not only feels included, but truly belongs.

Progress and Investments in DEI&B

Around 60 percent of companies have ramped up their financial and staffing investments in DEI&B. But the impact? Still not enough to create fair opportunities for women. Many organizations lack rigorous tracking and accountability for their DEI&B initiatives.

So, while we've made some headway, we're not there yet. It's time to dig deep, push harder, and make real, lasting changes.

Corporations that commit to championing DEI&B within their organizations can spark a wave of change that also bolsters their philanthropic efforts for women and girls and drives innovative solutions for a more equitable future.

Catherine Curry-Williams

Here's the scoop: research shows that small, consistent donations can have a massive impact.

(7)

Let's Get Practical:
$1.40 a Day = $5,000 Grant

I recently bought a cup of coffee, and to my surprise, it was five dollars—for a medium black Americano. Seriously, not a fancy latte with unicorn foam art. It wasn't even from some trendy spot, just your regular old coffee shop. This got me thinking about the power of small amounts of money and how $1.40 a day can actually make a difference.

Think about it—we can all live with one less coffee a day, right? Do the math. $1.40 a day adds up to $511 over a year. That's not chump change—it can be enough to buy a year's worth of school supplies, help fund a scholarship, or contribute to building safe housing for women in need. Imagine if everyone did the same—together, those small amounts could create a tidal wave of giving.

According to the Charities Aid Foundation, people who give small amounts regularly tend to donate more

Catherine Curry-Williams

overall than those who give large, one-time donations. It's like snacking throughout the day versus having one huge meal —you stay nourished longer with consistent snacking.

Picture your $1.40 as the secret ingredient in a recipe for change. Now, you might be thinking, "Okay, I get it. Small amounts add up. But why is it important to give strategically?"

Inspire
Definition: execute, encourage, or breathe life into.

Here's a quote I love (I have no clue where I heard it).

Inspiration needs both being inspired by something and then taking action on that inspiration.

This is exactly what your $1.40 a day can do—it's about getting inspired and then taking strategic action on that inspiration.

So, how do you make your $1.40 count? It starts with understanding what resonates with you. It means doing a bit of sleuthing on yourself.

Ask Yourself

- What are my priorities?
- What are my values?
- In what area do I want to see improvements? Gender inequity, housing, education, health?
- What really stands out in a charitable organization for me?
- Am I looking for organizations that aim to find long-term solutions to the community's problems that I'm interested in?
- Where did I first hear about charitable giving?
- Who influenced my views on philanthropy?
- What causes have I supported in the past, and why?
- How do I feel when I give to others?
- What kind of impact do I want my contributions to make?
- Do I prefer to support local causes, global initiatives, or a mix of both?
- How can I involve my friends and family in my philanthropic efforts?

Remember, $1.40 a day might seem like nothing, but when combined with intention and strategy, it becomes a powerful force for good. Get inspired, take action, and watch as your small contributions grow into something extraordinary.

And hey, remember what we talked about in Chapter 3? Finding that cool group of friends and starting a collective giving circle could take your $1.40 a day even further. Imagine pooling your resources with your besties, creating a super squad of do-gooders. You all chip in $1.40 a day, and suddenly, you've got a fund that's making serious waves. It's like turning your coffee money into a powerful punch of philanthropy.

Let's do the math again. If you and nine of your friends each contribute $1.40 a day, over a year, that's $5,110. That's a significant amount of money you can collectively give directly to an organization you all care about.

To make the message even more inspiring and to illustrate what $5,000 can do for a charity that mentors young girls to be leaders, here are some great examples.

Atlanta GLOW

Focuses on mentoring, leadership development, and life skills training for underserved young women. With $5,000, Atlanta GLOW could significantly enhance its one-on-one mentoring programs, provide additional leadership workshops, and expand its career readiness training to help young women prepare for and secure meaningful employment.

Girls Inc. of NYC

Delivers life-transforming programs that inspire girls to be strong, smart, and bold. With $5,000, Girls Inc. could sponsor several girls to participate in their comprehensive leadership programs, covering topics like economic literacy, healthy sexuality, and college preparedness.

Girls Who Code
Would use this size contribution to offer free summer programs that teach computer science skills to high school girls across the nation, helping bridge the gender gap in technology and empowering the next generation of female leaders.

True Beauty Discovery
Focusing on redefining beauty standards and boosting confidence among young girls through its Legendary Workshops. With $5000, they can host multiple one-day events for up to fifty girls, aged thirteen to eighteen, where they explore their strengths and capabilities through a creative framework and standards-based curriculum.

So, gather your crew, set some goals, and watch your impact multiply.

**You and your friends can spark real change
with just $1.40 a day.
Your collective effort will change lives.**

One of the greatest joys of philanthropy is the ability to live your values.

8

The Need, Here's Why

Living your values through philanthropy isn't just a duty; it can be a joy and a privilege. It's about seizing opportunities to make a meaningful impact. The opportunities are limitless, especially when supporting women through grassroots organizations. Being part of a philanthropic giving circle can provide an unparalleled opportunity to bring people together to make a real difference.

Whether it's supporting education, health care, economic empowerment, or leadership development, every contribution counts. Take the example of Malala Yousafzai, who used her Nobel Prize money to fund education for girls in Pakistan. Her foundation has helped countless girls access education, proving that strategic philanthropy can create lasting change.

Imagine the fulfillment that comes from knowing you've contributed to building a school, funding a scholarship, or supporting a women's shelter. For instance, a

Catherine Curry-Williams

woman in rural Kenya was able to start her own business selling handmade crafts thanks to a small grant from a grassroots organization. Her success transformed not only her life but also provided jobs for other women in her community. This is the joy and privilege of living your values.

The Importance of Mentorship

Mentorship in the workplace is particularly important for women and nonbinary people because of how much gender bias there is. People who aren't men have fewer opportunities, are paid less, and are trusted less. That can have a huge impact on a woman's confidence.

> ~Angela Rollins, Director of Financial
> Empowerment at the City of Rochester

The lack of female leaders makes it challenging to match ambitious women with mentors who have walked similar career paths. This is crucial because 80 percent of mentees prefer to be mentored by someone who has faced similar challenges. Men tend to choose mentees who look like them, exacerbating the disparity. Philanthropic efforts aimed at increasing female leadership can help bridge this gap by funding mentorship programs specifically designed for women.

But let's face it—living your values through philanthropy isn't just about serious stuff. It's about making a tangible, fun, and sometimes gritty impact on the world. It's about putting your money where your mouth is and seeing the change you wish to see. Remember the cool crew we talked about in Chapter 3? Yup, it's time to rally them again and dive deep into these causes.

Here's a quick lowdown on how philanthropy can seriously rock your world and the worlds of many women out there.

Economic Empowerment

Philanthropic donations can provide women with the resources they need to start their own businesses. For example, microloans and grants from organizations like Kiva have helped countless women in developing countries launch small enterprises, lifting themselves and their families out of poverty.

Picture this—a woman goes from selling crafts at a local market to running a thriving business, all because of a little financial boost.

Education

Scholarships and educational programs funded by philanthropic efforts open doors for women and girls that would otherwise remain closed. For instance, the Malala Fund works to ensure girls worldwide have access to twelve years of free, safe, and quality education, empowering them to achieve their dreams.

Imagine being the reason a girl in a remote village gets to wear a graduation cap and walk across that stage—priceless!

Health Care

Philanthropic support for health care initiatives can lead to better health outcomes for women and girls. Organizations like the Global Fund for Women provide grants to grassroots groups that deliver essential health services, including maternal care and reproductive health education.

Leadership Development

Programs designed to develop women's leadership skills are vital. The Women's Leadership Development Initiative, funded by various philanthropic organizations, focuses on training women in leadership roles and thereby increasing their representation in various sectors.

Imagine being part of the force that brings more women into boardrooms, politics, and other high-impact areas.

I know I keep circling back to similar themes throughout this book, but it's because they're so important. All of these contributions aren't just helping others—they're enriching your life, too. When you live your values through giving, you're creating a legacy of compassion and change.

So, grab your squad, brainstorm some awesome ideas, and dive into the world of philanthropy. It's not just about changing lives—it's about living your values out loud and proud. Get out there, make a splash, and watch as your efforts turn ripples into waves of change.

Philanthropy isn't just for the super rich; it's for anyone with a big heart and the desire to make a difference.

Catherine Curry-Williams

Your Change-Maker's Toolkit

I've left blank pages for you to jot down your thoughts, goals, and action plans. Use them to dream big, plan your next steps, and reflect on your journey. Write your own story of change and make it an epic one.

Your Goals: List what you want to achieve.

_____

_____

_____

_____

_____

_____

_____

_____

Catherine Curry-Williams

Your Squad: Write down the names of friends and family who will join you in your philanthropic journey.

_____

_____

_____

_____

_____

_____

_____

_____

_____

_____

_____

_____

_____

_____

_____

_____

_____

_____

_____

Action Plan: Outline your steps to make an impact.

_____

_____

_____

_____

_____

_____

_____

_____

_____

_____

_____

_____

_____

_____

_____

_____

_____

_____

_____

_____

_____

Catherine Curry-Williams

Inspirations: Keep track of the causes and stories that inspire you.

_____

_____

_____

_____

_____

_____

_____

_____

_____

_____

_____

_____

_____

_____

_____

_____

_____

_____

_____

_____

_____

Organizations you've supported in the past. And why.

_____

_____

_____

_____

_____

_____

_____

_____

_____

_____

_____

_____

_____

_____

_____

_____

_____

_____

_____

Catherine Curry-Williams

Causes you're passionate about and think need more attention in your community or globally.

_____

_____

_____

_____

_____

_____

_____

_____

_____

_____

_____

_____

_____

_____

_____

_____

_____

_____

_____

_____

_____

Believe in Yourself

Use this space to affirm your commitment to creating positive change. Write down mantras or affirmations that inspire you to keep pushing forward. Here are a few to get you started:

- I am a force for good in the world.
- My contributions, no matter how small, make a difference.
- I attract like-minded individuals who share my passion for change.
- I have the power to create a better future.
- Together, we can turn ripples into waves of transformation.

Remember, you've got this.
The world is ready for your impact.
Go out there and make it happen.

_____

_____

_____

_____

_____

_____

_____

_____

Catherine Curry-Williams

Catherine Curry-Williams

Every single act of giving, no matter how small, contributes to a bigger picture.

(10)

The Final Push—Your Legacy of Change

Here we are, at the end of this journey, but really, it's just the beginning. You've navigated through the ins and outs of philanthropy, discovered the power of collective giving, and learned how small actions can lead to big changes. Now, it's time to take all that knowledge and passion and turn it into a legacy of change.

Remember, philanthropy isn't just for the billionaires with their names on shiny plaques. It's for anyone who cares enough to make a difference. And guess what? That includes you.

Think back to that $1.40 a day we talked about. It might seem like a tiny drop in the ocean, but as we've seen, those drops can create ripples, and those ripples can turn into waves.

Now, let's kick it up a notch. Imagine you're on a mission to save the world—because, in many ways, you are. This isn't about being perfect or having it all figured out. It's about showing up, doing the work, and making a difference. It's about getting your hands dirty, facing challenges head-on, and not being afraid to shake things up.

Your Call to Action

So, what's next? Here's where you get to take everything you've learned and put it into action. Here are a few gritty, no-nonsense steps to get you started.

1

Set Your Goals
What do you want to achieve? Whether it's supporting education for girls, improving healthcare, or empowering women entrepreneurs, set clear, actionable goals. Write them down, and don't be afraid to aim high.

2

Build Your Team
Remember that awesome squad we talked about? Gather your friends, family, and anyone else who shares your passion. Create a collective giving circle, brainstorm ideas, and pool your resources. Together, you're unstoppable.

3

Get Involved
Don't just write checks. Get out there and volunteer. See the impact of your efforts firsthand. Whether it's mentoring young women, building houses, or organizing community events, your

time and energy are invaluable.

4 Raise Awareness

Use your voice. Talk about the causes you care about on social media, at work, and with your friends. Spread the word and inspire others to join the movement. Remember, awareness is just as powerful as money.

5 Stay Committed

Philanthropy isn't a one-time deal. It's a lifelong commitment. Keep pushing, keep striving, and keep giving. When you hit obstacles—and you will—remember why you started and keep going.

Believe in Your Impact

I know I've hammered this point home, but it's worth repeating—your contributions matter.

Think about the stories you've read in this book—the woman in Kenya who started her own business, the girls in Pakistan who got an education thanks to Mala-

You have the power to make a real, tangible difference. Don't let anyone tell you otherwise.

la's foundation, the countless women who've found their voices and strength through grassroots movements. These are real people whose lives were changed because someone like you decided to care and take action.

Your Legacy

At the end of the day, it's all about the legacy you leave behind. What kind of world do you want to create? What impact do you want to have? This is your chance to shape the future, to be remembered as someone who made a difference.

So, here's your final challenge—go out there and be the change-maker you were born to be. Use your passion, your grit, and your humor to inspire others.

Turn those ripples into waves and create a legacy of compassion, empowerment, and lasting change.

Author's Note

Thank you from the bottom of my heart for reading this book. Your time, attention, and willingness to join this journey mean the world to me. Let's make a difference, one small step at a time.

Please be kind to yourself and remember that change doesn't happen overnight. It takes time, effort, and perseverance; eventually, you'll see the impact of your efforts.

Margaret Mead (1901-1978) was a prominent American cultural anthropologist known for her studies and works on the impact of culture on personality and human behavior. Margaret Mead was a vocal supporter of civil rights, women's rights, and environmental conservation. Her famous quote about the power of small groups of committed citizens reflects her belief in the capacity of individuals and communities to effect meaningful social change.

"Never doubt that a small group of thoughtful, committed citizens can change the world. Indeed, it is the only thing that ever has."

Acknowledgments

To my mom—your endless giving and boundless love continue to inspire me every day, even though you're no longer with us. Your lessons on generosity have kept me grounded and driven.

To Scott Williams— I'm grateful for all of the wonderful years together and for our children Shane and Grace.

To my daughter, Grace, who reminds me every day of what truly matters. You give me the fuel to keep pushing for a planet that's better for all.

To my sisters—Cheryl Gabriel, Cheri Harvey, Karen Brown, Peri Bresnick—you've backed me in everything I've tackled. Your support means the world.

To Marilyn Kentz—forever supporting, coaching, and directing me to find the highest good. Your friend-

Catherine Curry-Williams

ship and guidance have been invaluable.

To Liz Svatek, thank you for making me push the limits when it came to a TED talk and championing my efforts to take it further by writing this book.

To the incredible women in my women's group: Deborah Brooks, Jill Mullikin-Bates, Ramey Warren, Stefanie Novik, and Minda Burr. For twenty years, you have helped me find my true north. Our journey has more to go, and I couldn't be more grateful to do it with all of you.

And to my amazing friends, my tribe of earth angels— Sabrina Spagnolo, Joan Ryan, Dougal Fraser, David Harel, Dr. Theresa Ashby, Carla Pennington, Robin Radin, Hillary Smith, Randy Thomas, Lynn Ferguson, Barbara Deutch, Phyllis Spagnolo, Cheryl Benton, Carrie Murray, Nita Whitaker, Leslie Bonar, Daryl Twerdahl, for always being there and going above and beyond the call of duty every time I ask. Without your laughter and your kick-in-the-pants encouragement, this book, my thoughts—they'd all just be whispers in the wind.

My heart is full of love and gratitude.

About the Author

For over two decades, Catherine Curry-Williams has challenged conventional concepts of philanthropy affecting change and leaving an indelible mark on individuals and communities worldwide. As the founder of Shane's Inspiration, established in 1997 in memory of her son, she and the team have led global initiatives to create inclusive playgrounds, uniting children of all abilities. She expanded her impact by cofounding She Angels Foundation, which awards monthly grants to grassroots organizations supporting women and girls. A fervent advocate for women's empowerment, she shares her wisdom and passion through mentoring and speaking. Her impactful journey has earned her prestigious awards, including recognition as one of L'Oreal Paris's Women of Worth and the Lifetime Achievement Award from President Barack Obama.

The proceeds from this book will be donated to:

Inclusion Matters by Shane's Inspiration
https://inclusionmatters.org/

She Angels Foundation
https://sheangelsfoundation.org

Catherine Curry-Williams

Grassroots
Organizations
to
Check Out

Addendum

- **A Moment of Magic** https://amomentofmagic.org
- **Ann Bancroft Foundation** https://AnnBancroftfoundation.org
- **Bay Area Girls Club** https://bagirlsclub.org
- **Bella Abzug Leadership Institute** https://www.abzuginstitute.org/
- **Bio Girls** https://www.biogirls.org/
- **Dear NICU MAMA** https://www.dearnicumama.com/mission
- **DemocraShe** https://democrashe.org
- **Every Day Action** https://youreverydayaction.org
- **Exposher, Inc.** https://exposherinc.org
- **Girls Who Read, Inc.** https://girlswhoread.org
- **Global Women in Blockchain** https://globalwomeninblockchain.org
- **GreenLight Women** https://greenlightwomen.org
- **Her Vaga Bound Roots** https://hervagaboundroots.com

- **Inclusion Matters by Shane's Inspiration**
  https://inclusionmatters.org
- **Jeremiah program** https://jeremiahprogram.org/
- **Love Life Now** https://lovelifenow.org
- **Maestra Music** https://maestramusic.org
- **My Sister's Keeper Success Institute**
  https://msksi.com
- **New York Milk Bank** https://nymilkbank.org
- **No Limits for Deaf Children**
  https://nolimitsfordeafchildren.org
- **People's Pottery Project**
  https://peoplespotteryproject.com
- **Project Dot** https://projectdot.org
- **PS I Love You Foundation**
  https://psiloveyoufoundation.org
- **She Is Hope LA** https://sheishopela.org
- **She TV Media** https://shetv.me
- **SixDegrees** https://www.sixdegrees.org/about
- **St. Anne's Family Services** https://stannes.org
- **Statement Junky** http://statementjunky.org
- **Take My Hand Girl** https://takemyhandgirl.com
- **Teach AAPI** https://teachaapi.org
- **Teen Leadership Foundation**
  https://teenleadershipfoundation.com
- **The L-Project** https://thelproject.org

- **The Ovarian Cancer Circle**
  https://theovariancancercircle.org

- **The Women's Empowerment Network**
  https://thewennetwork.org

- **The Women's Resource**
  https://womensresourcecenter.net

- **True Beauty Discovery**
  https://truebeautydiscovery.org

- **We Spark Cancer Support Center**
  https://wespark.org

- **Wings World Quest** https://wingsworldquest.org

- **WISEPlace** https://wiseplace.org

- **Women Founders Network**
  https://womenfoundersnetwork.org

- **Women in Media** https://womennmedia.com

- **Women Veterans Giving**
  https://womenveteransgiving.org

- **Women's Impact** https://womensimpactinc.com

- **Women's Fund of Hawaii**
  https://womensfundhawaii.org

Catherine Curry-Williams

Made in the USA
Columbia, SC
14 September 2024

42313281R00054